Origami & Papercraft

PAPER DECORATIONS

ARCTURUS

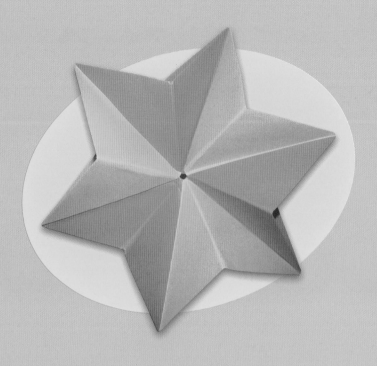

This edition first published in 2015 by Arcturus Publishing

Distributed by Black Rabbit Books
P.O. Box 3263
Mankato
Minnesota MN 56002

Models and photography: Jessica Moon
Text: Jennifer Sanderson
Editors: Becca Clunes and Joe Harris
Designer: Jessica Moon

Library of Congress Cataloging-in-Publication Data

Sanderson, Jennifer, author.
 Paper decorations / Jennifer Sanderson and Jessica Moon.
     pages cm. -- (Origami and papercraft)
 Audience: Grades 4 to 6.
 Includes bibliographical references and index.
 ISBN 978-1-78404-084-0
1. Origami--Juvenile literature. 2. Paper work--Juvenile literature. 3. Holiday decorations--Juvenile
literature. 4. Decoration and ornament--Juvenile literature. I. Moon, Jessica, designer. II. Title.
 TT872.5.S2635 2015
 736.982--dc23

                                     2013048248

Printed in China

SL004078US
Supplier 29, Date 0514, Print Run 3406

Contents

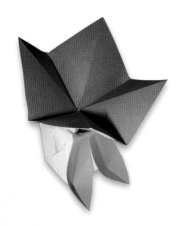
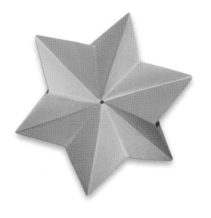

Introduction

Origami has been popular in Japan for hundreds of years and is now loved all around the world. You can make great models with just one sheet of paper and this book shows you how!

The paper used in origami is thin but strong, so that it can be folded many times. It is usually colored on one side. Alternatively, you can use ordinary scrap paper but make sure it's not too thick.

Origami models often share the same folds and basic designs, known as "bases". This introduction explains some of the folds and bases that you will need for the projects in this book. When making the models, follow the key below to find out what the lines and arrows mean. Always crease your paper well!

MOUNTAIN FOLD

To make a mountain fold, fold the paper so that the crease is pointing up toward you, like a mountain.

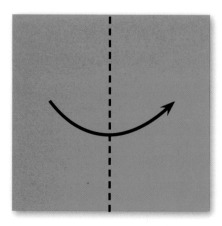
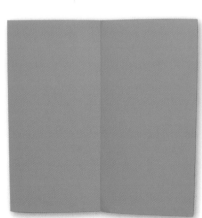

VALLEY FOLD

To make a valley fold, fold the paper the other way, so that the crease is pointing away from you, like a valley.

INSIDE REVERSE FOLD

An inside reverse fold is useful if you want to flatten the shape of part of your model.

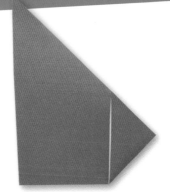

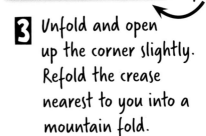

Open

1 Practice by first folding a piece of paper diagonally in half. Make a valley fold on one point and crease.

2 It's important to make sure that the paper is creased well. Run your finger over the crease two or three times.

3 Unfold and open up the corner slightly. Refold the crease nearest to you into a mountain fold.

4 Open up the paper a little more and then tuck the tip of the point inside. This is the view from the underside of the paper. Close the paper.

5 Flatten the paper. You now have an inside reverse fold.

KEY

valley fold `-------------------------`	direction to move paper
mountain fold `·························`	direction to push or pull
step fold (mountain and valley fold next to each other)	

WATERBOMB BASE

1 Start with a square of paper, with the point toward you. Make two diagonal valley folds.

2 The paper should now look like this. Turn it over.

3 Make two valley folds along the horizontal and vertical lines.

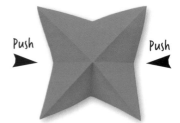

Push   Push

4 Push the paper into this shape, so the center spot pops up.

5 Push in the sides, so that the back and front sections are brought together.

6 Flatten the paper. You now have a waterbomb base.

SQUARE BASE

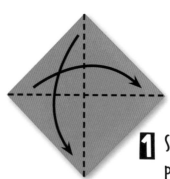

1 Start with the point turned toward you. Valley fold diagonally both ways.

2 The paper should look like this. Now turn it over.

3 Valley fold along the horizontal and vertical lines.

4 The paper should now look like this. Turn it so that one of the points is facing you.

5 Hold the paper by opposite diagonal corners. Push the two corners together so that the shape begins to collapse.

6 Flatten the top of the paper into a square shape. You now have a square base.

BLINTZ BASE

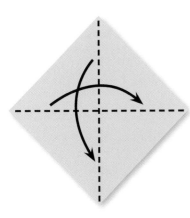

1 Start with a square of paper, with the point toward you. Make two diagonal valley folds.

2 The paper should now look like this. Fold the bottom point up to the center.

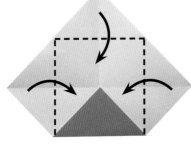

3 Repeat step 2 with the three remaining points.

4 You now have a blintz base.

Super Star

Perfect to brighten up any celebration, this star looks complicated but it's really easy to make!

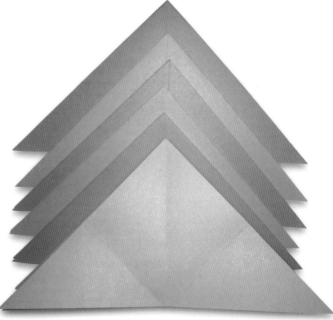

Wow!

START WITH SIX WATERBOMB BASES

1 Place your first waterbomb base so the open part is at the bottom. Valley fold the left side up to the center point, crease well, and unfold.

2 Valley fold the right side up to the center point, crease well, and unfold. Turn over and repeat steps 1 and 2 on the reverse side.

3 You now have one section of your star. Repeat steps 1 and 2 on the five remaining waterbomb bases.

4 Once you have your six sections you are ready to assemble your star.

◀ Slide

Close-up of
interlocking points.

5 Start with two sections. Slide the left points
of the right piece of paper into the right
points of the left piece of paper. The two
pieces should interlock. Slide the points in
as far as they will go.

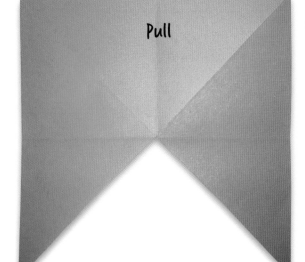
Pull

6 Your two sections should
now look like this. Pull
the center fold out to
shape your star. Repeat
on the reverse.

7 Your two sections should now look like this. Repeat steps 5 and 6 with the remaining sections, adding them one at a time to your sections already added. Finish your star by slotting the last section into the first section, using steps 5 and 6 as a guide.

DID YOU KNOW?
The closest star to Earth (besides the Sun) is 4.2 light-years away. It would take you more than 70,000 years to get there!

8
Your star is ready! Use it as a decoration for parties and special occasions.

Table Flower

A set table will be complete with this table decoration in place. If the table is long, make three or four to put down the length of the table.

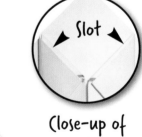

So sweet!

START WITH A WATERBOMB BASE

1 Choose green paper if you can. Make sure the colored side of your waterbomb base is on the inside.

2 Valley fold the left and right points of the top flaps up into the center.

3 Valley fold the left and right sides into the center.

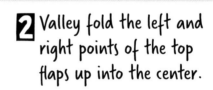

Slot

Close-up of pockets.

4 Valley fold the top points down into the center.

5 Slot the points into the pockets of the side triangles.

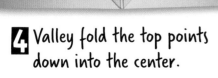

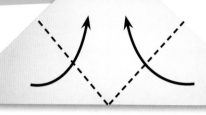

6 Your model should now look like this. Turn it over.

7 Valley fold the left and right points up into the center.

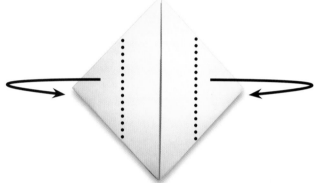

8 Mountain fold the left and right sides back into the center.

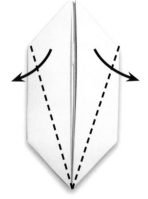

9 Valley fold the left and right flaps out to the sides.

Pull   Pull

10 To create the leaves of your table decoration, gently pull the sides toward you to open them out.

11 Mountain fold the bottom point, crease well, and unfold.

Blow here

12 Your model should now look like this. Carefully blow into the gap at the bottom. Your model should start to inflate. If you need to, use your fingers to gently pull out the sides.

13 Your model should now look like this. Put it to one side and get another piece of paper to make the flower.

START WITH A SQUARE BASE

14 Start with a square base, making sure your colored side is on the inside and the open part is at the bottom.

15 Valley fold the top left and right sides into the center. Turn your paper over and repeat on the reverse.

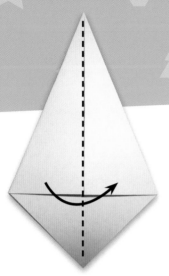

16 Fold the left side over to the right side.

17 Valley fold the top point down at an angle.

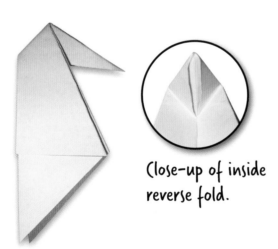

Close-up of inside reverse fold.

18 Turn this fold into an inside reverse fold to create your flower stem. See page 5 if you need help.

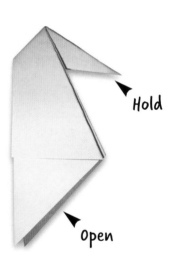

Hold

Open

19 Hold onto the stem and gently unfold each point to create the petals. Use your finger to flatten them.

20 Your model should now look like this.

Insert stem

21 Now insert the flower stem into the hole on the top of your base to complete your decoration.

22 Your pretty flower is ready and will look lovely on any table.

Christmas Wreath

At Christmastime, many people put wreaths on their front doors. You could put your wreath on your bedroom door to get into the Christmas spirit.

START WITH YOUR PAPER COLORED SIDE DOWN

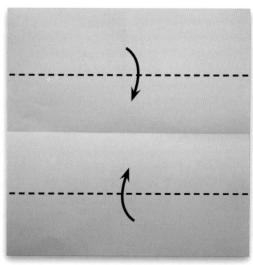

Very merry!

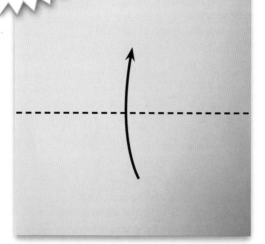

1 Valley fold your paper in half from bottom to top, crease well and then unfold.

2 Valley fold the top and bottom sections into the center.

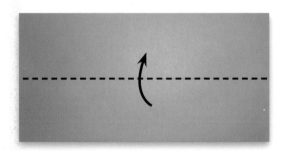

3 Valley fold your paper in half upward so that the open side is at the top.

4 Valley fold down the left and right corners.

5 Valley fold your paper in half from right to left in the middle.

DID YOU KNOW?
Christmas wreaths are traditionally made from evergreen leaves to last throughout the winter.

6 Your model should look like this. Repeat steps 1 to 5 on new paper 7 times so that you have 8 pieces in total. Use different colors to make your wreath more colorful.

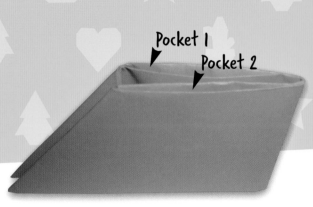

Pocket 1
Pocket 2

7 To put your wreath together, start with two pieces. Take the first piece and hold it by the triangle ends and turn it so you can see the two pockets at the top.

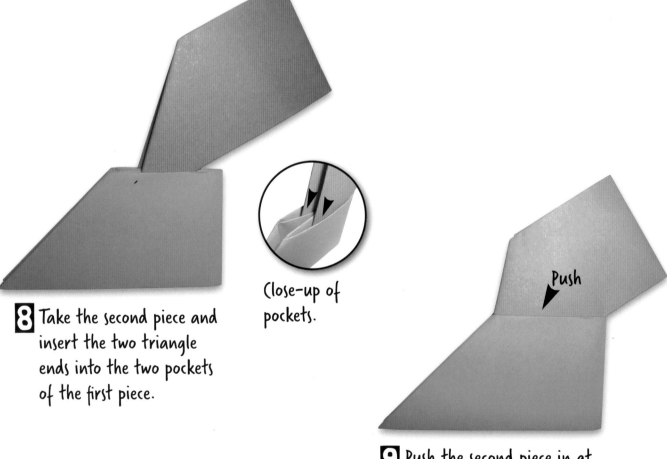

8 Take the second piece and insert the two triangle ends into the two pockets of the first piece.

Close-up of pockets.

Push

9 Push the second piece in at an angle as far as it will go. Repeat this step with the third piece and so on.

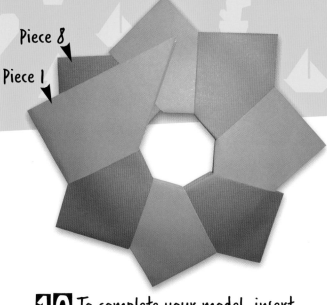

Piece 8

Piece 1

10 To complete your model, insert the triangle ends of the first piece into the pockets of the eighth piece.

11 When your wreath is ready, you could decorate it by tying a lovely ribbon to it.

Photo Frame

Put a picture of friends or your pet in this pretty photo frame. It will certainly brighten up any room.

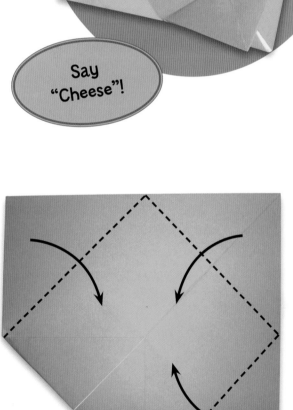

Say "Cheese"!

START WITH A BLINTZ BASE

1 Put your blintz base flap-side down. Valley fold the left point into the center.

2 Do the same with the three remaining points.

3 Turn your model so that one corner is pointing toward you. It should now look like this.

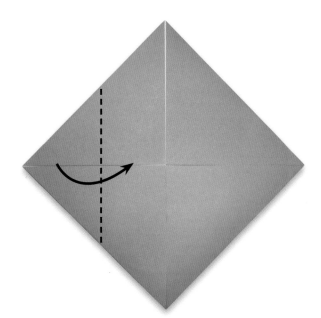

4 Turn your model over and valley fold the left point into the center.

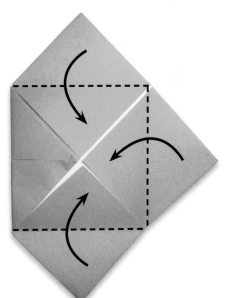

5 Repeat step 4 with the three remaining points.

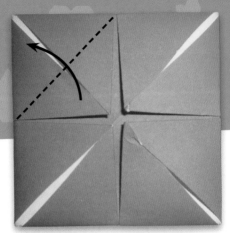

6 Turn over your model and valley fold the top left flap out to the top left corner.

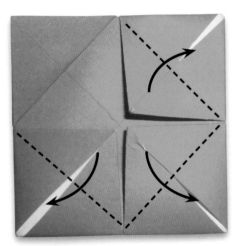

7 Do the same with the three remaining flaps.

Insert photo

8 Insert your photo into the frame by slotting it into the corners.

DID YOU KNOW?
The oldest surviving photograph was taken around 1826 by the French inventor Joseph Niépce.

 Use the bottom flap at the back of your frame to stand the frame up.

10
Your frame is now ready to display. You could make one for each member of your family!

Winter Icicle

Transform any room into a winter wonderland by making lots of these icicles. You could even attach string to them and hang them.

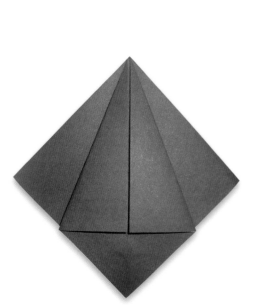

Brrrr!

START
WITH A
SQUARE
BASE

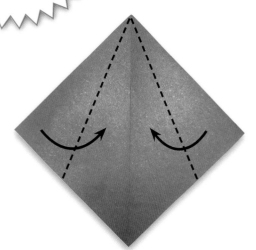

1 Turn your square base so that the open end is facing downward. Valley fold the left and right sides into the center.

2 Turn your paper over and repeat step 1 on the reverse.

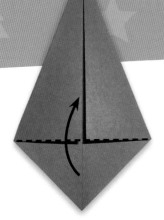

3 Your model should now look like this. Valley fold the top layer of the bottom flap up and crease well.

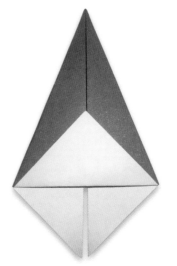

4 Turn your paper over and repeat step 3 on the reverse.

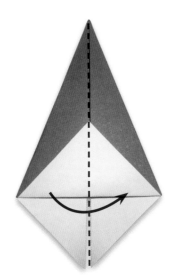

5 Valley fold the paper in the middle, crease well, and then unfold.

6 Take a second piece of paper and repeat steps 1 to 5 to create a second section.

7 Turn the second section so that the narrow end is pointing downward. Valley fold the top right flap over to the left.

8 Your model should now look like this. Turn your paper over and repeat the valley fold from step 7 on the reverse.

Slot

Slot

Close-up of front and back sides.

Close-up of left and right sides.

Close-up of sections slotting together.

9 Slide your fingers inside each section to open them out a bit, then carefully slot the two sections together, tucking the colored points behind the white triangles to hold the model in place.

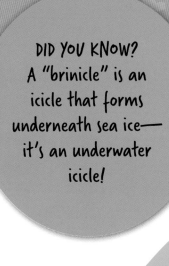

DID YOU KNOW?
A "brinicle" is an icicle that forms underneath sea ice— it's an underwater icicle!

10

Your icicle decoration is now ready. If you make more icicles, keep to shades of blue and white for an icy look.

Flower

This pretty flower will last for ever. Why not make several and surprise someone with a lovely bouquet of flowers?

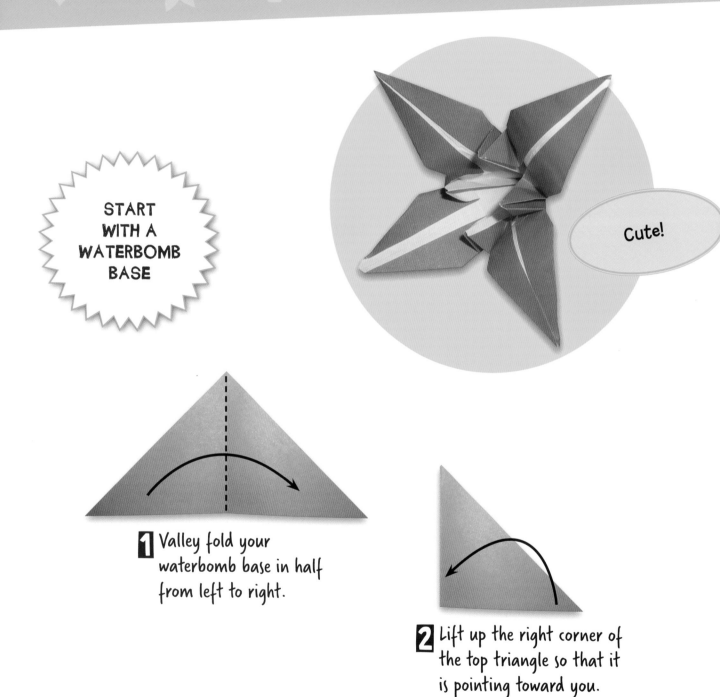

START WITH A WATERBOMB BASE

Cute!

1 Valley fold your waterbomb base in half from left to right.

2 Lift up the right corner of the top triangle so that it is pointing toward you.

3 Press it down in the center to flatten it.

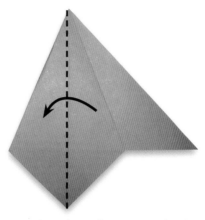

4 Your model should now look like this. Fold the right side over to the left and repeat steps 2 and 3 on the remaining three triangles until they are all flattened.

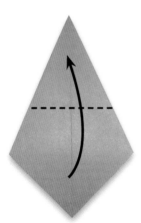

5 Your model should now look like this. Make sure you have the same number of flaps on each side, then valley fold the whole model in half, crease well, and unfold.

6 Valley fold the top left and right sides into the center, crease well, and unfold.

7 Lift the bottom point of the upper layer to meet the top point.

8 Your model should look like this. Valley fold in the left and right sides at the top along the creases made in step 6 and flatten them.

9 Your model should look like this. Repeat steps 7 and 8 on the remaining three sides.

10 Valley fold the top points down on all four sides.

11 Your model should now look like this. Turn your model so that the open points at the bottom are at the top.

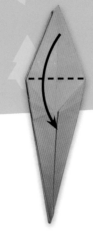

12 Valley fold the left and right sides into the center.

13 Repeat step 12 on the remaining three sides.

14 Your paper should now look like this. Valley fold down the four sides to open up the petals.

15 Now that your flower is complete, why not use different colored paper to make a whole bouquet?

Glossary

base A simple, folded shape that is used as the starting point for many different origami projects.

blintz base An origami shape named after a thin pancake and formed by folding all four corners of a paper square to the center point.

evergreen A plant that has green leaves all year.

mountain fold An origami step where a piece of paper is folded so that the crease is pointing upwards, like a mountain.

valley fold An origami step where a piece of paper is folded so that the crease is pointing downwards, like a valley.

waterbomb A traditional origami shape, which can be filled with water.

Further Reading

Absolute Beginner's Origami by Nick Robinson (Potter Craft, 2006)

My First Origami Book by Susan Akass (CICO Kidz, 2011)

Party Origami by Jessica Okui (Chronicle, 2013)

World's Best Origami by Nick Robinson (Alpha Books, 2010)

Web Sites

www.origami-fun.com/ A fun origami web site that features free, printable pdfs for every project on the site. Several pages are devoted to seasonal decorations.

en.origami-club.com/ An extensive web site devoted to origami. The instructions for each project can be viewed as a diagram or an animation. It includes pages for special occasions, such as Halloween and Valentine's Day.

Index